NVivo 12

In 7 Steps

Qualitative Data Analysis and Coding for Researchers

Dr. Troy Looney

Dr. Troy Looney

Copyright © 2018 Dr. Troy Looney

ISBN: **10: 1727381939**
ISBN-13: **978-1727381931**

DEDICATION

To every scholar that seeks to emerge to

Into their higher self in academia.

Thank you.

Press forward!

Be the Change Agent!

NVIVO 12 CONTENTS

ACKNOWLEDGMENTS

I acknowledge QSR International for developing such a wonderful tool for use in qualitative research. You have enabled me to learn a new skill set that has allowed me to help many scholars all over the world. Thank you for continued effort and support to give us an essential element and tool to analyze data with efficiency. The saga continues as we each evolve and learn infinitely.

WHAT IS NVIVO SOFTWARE?

NVIVO 12 is the updated data coding software that was created by QSR International for analyzing data collected for qualitative studies, with added features. Researchers are encouraged to use NVIVO 12 software to evaluate, interpret, and explain any social phenomena. The NVIVO 12 software has been enhanced to engage qualitative research, and mixed methods research in development. NVIVO 12 has added a significant amount of features that will support the development of data analysis when performing semi structured interviews, surveys, web pages, field notes, and journal articles during data collection.

Researchers are able to evaluate, acquisition, and interpret qualitative data centered on their research question(s). The interview questions of an open-ended nature are structured to explore the descriptive data that asks the how and why questions from participants. NVIVO 12 allows you to organize, manage, and aggregate data in a qualitative study to develop categories initially, coded data, and ultimately complete the refinement of coding data for the essence of thematic analysis.

THEMATIC ANALYSIS

Thematic analysis is a very common method of data analysis in qualitative research. As required by every researcher, the process of thematic analysis is performed through inductive and deductive reasoning to identify patterned meanings or themes within groups of data (Braun, Clarke, & Terry, 2014). According to Braun, Clarke, & Terry (2014) the analysis is the process of discovering themes that are already existing in data sets. In earlier versions of the NVIVO data coding software; the process of executing the data analysis was outlined in detailed recommendations.

These previous steps were outlined as follows: 1) import, 2) explore, 3) code, 4) query, 5) reflect, 6) visualize, 7) memo. Each of these steps are recommended for how to code and analyze your data for research. It is important to find your themes and patterns for the emerging data. NVIVO 12 also offers the introduction of assessing and adding elements of quantitative research to support a mixed methods style of research.

WHAT IS DATA CODING?

Data coding is the act of organizing data by topic, theme, or case descriptions that are saved in the NVIVO 12 software as container folders in the software program. The data can be imported in several formats and from several various sources such as: pdf files, word documents, audio files, datasets, videos, and pictures. The "Nodes" that were mentioned are folders that allow us to organize, manage and arrange the data for examining the data and its emerging thematic elements based on participant responses. After all of the data has been imported, you will save the data in the proper folder location (now the FILES folder). Coding your data provides you the ability to have the categorization and separation of the data into sets that you can quickly and easily access for evaluation. The coded words, phrases, and elements of interest are aligned within the context of themes for you to explore, interpret, and evaluate as needed. The benefit of coding is in the aggregating of data for later comparison and contrasting during the write up portion of your research study. Data coding with NVIVO 12 allows you to better manage and control the datasets that you organize.

THE NODES

The raw data that you input into the software are divided by participant responses from interviews. As your themes begin to emerge, NVIVO 12 offers you the NODES as containers to hold every initial context of themes in categories of interest. The NODES folder will be where you drag and drop the coded phrases and words to, but for now let's continue with the process of how we engage the data by hand (manually). The software also maintains a detailed count of references made by all of the participants in your data collection.

CODING BY HAND (MANUALLY)

When we talk about coding manually, we mean the process of you the researchers, actually looking at the data page by page, and interpreting the meaning and context of each phrase, word, and text query that exists within the data sets. This is the process, by which you become very connected to the data, and you are able to understand the data more intimately. This process, is required for researchers at several stages of the data collection and analysis subsequently anyhow. Of course I have talked with many colleagues that decided to initiate their data coding by hand, and it took them much longer to complete. The coding by hand is fine to introduce and even complete, however; many universities are now requiring some type of data coding software to at least check your work and to better manage the process with software. When you code by hand, you are actively engaging with your data, similarly to having transcribed every interview, as I did myself. You may find the process of transcribing your own data, more engaging based on the repetitiveness. It is through these repetitions, that these data provides us with closer connectivity to the deeper meanings. Do not be afraid to engage the data with academic rigor. You are completing a level of scholarly work that is considered timeless.

THE DIFFERENCE

The difference with coding by hand and coding with NVIVO 12 is that you have software that can aggregate your data, with more features. You are still the analytical expert for your data, and you should manually check it after the NVIVO 12 coding process. The NVIVO 12 software can analyze keywords and phrases, while also recognizing word and text frequencies through running specific queries. NVIVO 12 then calculates these data and provides very detailed reference and summary links to list the content by nodes. The Nodes are also categorized by how each participant responded to each Topic, which will later be refined into the final themes of meaning. Those specific responses are the data that have been coded into each node, under the specific category. We first will create the categories and topics, then later refine the data in context overall.

THE SEVEN STEPS

The seven steps used in this book were selected from my actual use of NVIVO 12 software and my experience during exploring my data with how I decided to best approach the coding and data analysis using NVIVO 12 software. The steps that I selected for use are now aligned and improved as these steps allow you to 1) coding data responses, 2) review the coding, 3) text & word queries, 4) analysis of the data, 5) refined themes for writing, 6) demographics with NVIVO 12, and 7) additional analysis required. As I mentioned, the steps were initially used to manage and analyze my interview data after data collection was completed. These steps worked for my successful process of coding and analysis as did my original data protocol, but as with everything, it's ok to evolve and become fully aware if all new versions and features. Since I successfully utilized these steps in my coding process, you too should consider the use of these steps to keep the process very simple and orderly. There is no industry standard process for taking steps in qualitative data coding and support. In the former NVIVO *Getting Started* guide, the NVIVO literature had seven steps as well. In the former NVIVO versions, these steps were identified as 1) import, 2) explore, 3) code, 4) query, 5) reflect, 6) visualize, 7) memo. The steps in the *Getting Started* guide were very closely aligned with my seven steps that I had originally developed, before ever seeing the guide. This was coincidental in nature and it was very unique in that the first book had been written before I discovered the NVIVO Getting Started Guide. This original process was also completed before the NVIVO in 7 Steps book was released. This confirms that while there is no set industry standard for how to approach data coding, the QSR International developers of NVIVO software agreed with me in theory and approach.

THE NVIVO TOOL

The process works in several steps. Primarily 7 Steps! This book was written as a guide to show NVIVO as a tool to support doctoral students and researchers in the data coding and analysis phase while pursuing a dissertation study. NVIVO is just a tool; however, it is very supportive if you learn how to effectively use the NVIVO tool. You must become the artist to use and learn it most effectively. This book provides the context of how to approach the NVIVO 12 software with a direct and clear understanding on using the software most effectively. As I offered my coaching and consulting services to several clients and students that were pursuing their doctoral studies; I was approached and asked to help several people that were totally frustrated by having to learn the NVIVO software.

SUPPORT OTHERS

It is imperative to offer your help to others, as I too had some helpful mentors throughout my doctoral journey. I understood how important it was to offer your wealth of knowledge at this stage of the doctoral journey, and even earlier on in the program. Being that I had a great experience in learning and developing my own system of NVIVO data coding and analysis, the notes and steps that I conducted were important to recollect and write out for others. This book should be utilized as a guide and reference tool for review and now even expands the process into data analysis. The most valuable advice offered is in the idea that you don't have to make it complicated, but try to be very direct in your needs and steps taken toward getting the analysis and data coding done, but not only that, but actually understanding the process and why it makes sense.

WHAT'S NEW IN NVIVO 12?

We have discussed what NVIVO 11 Data Coding Software is, so let's talk about how NVIVO 12 software is different from NVIVO 11. I used NVIVO 11 for the past few years, and it has worked well for me. **So here are the major differences:**

- NVIVO 12 software has improved methods for learning to use the software.

- Improved methods of visualizations and exporting for presentations, and report generations.

- Streamlined options to manage cases and demographical data

- Crosstabs analysis to manage attributes and mixed methods analyses.

- Use the NCapture add-on to gather social media content for analysis and inclusion into the research process.

- Exchange data with Mixed Methods tools such as IBM SPSS, Excel, and Access.

- Take your content Mobile with Evernote connectivity, and more…

INTRODUCING NEW ELEMENTS

The new elements of NVIVO 12 data coding software are very similar to the former versions. This is so much more than a You Tube video can offer. I know because I developed my system to get you done quickly. You can use the former versions of NVIVO to code your data with the very same efficiency, but you will have more options to assist you with NVIVO 12. I am here to help you fellow colleagues and grad students! First; thank you for the purchase and taking the time to consider the simple and direct way to getting your coding and analysis done with NVIVO 12 software. If you are like me as a student, then time is of the essence; funding is extremely low; and you need to GET THIS CODING DONE! The key is to do it right the first time. Of course even if you are challenged, then it can be corrected. I have been there and done that! So that is exactly what we are going to do. Take a breath and exhale. This data coding and analysis process will be one of the most rewarding parts of the doctoral journey in the research portion. Well, let me correct that. I enjoyed the interview portion, and this is a continuation of that process! Yes, I chose to use short paragraphs, and I will be very concise about "NVIVO 12 in 7 STEPS". This edition is very similar to the original book, except we will highlight the changes and I have added some new elements for your analysis considerations.

THE CHALLENGE

In very similar 7 Steps, and you will be done coding all of that wonderful transcribed data that you spent so much time accumulating. Ok. So this book is for qualitative researchers, and you will enjoy this process as I did. It is very challenging, but it will serve you well in understanding the data. I have found my method to the madness and I am here to share it with you. The important thing to remember is that data analysis and coding is not like computer coding or writing a complex program for Microsoft or an algorithm. This coding is the data management and about having a system of management for your data. The participants were de-identified and coded by number or lettering in the interview process. The data coding will be by categories, then subsequently refined into the more significant thematic elements after managing the data in the NVIVO 12 software. NVIVO 12, or any other previous version, is just a tool for us to use, as we still have to interpret the data to make sense of its meaning.

THE PROCESS

Consider this a continuation of that protection and confidentiality for the many wonderful participants that agreed to help us reach this status. I was happy when I actually had some data to analyze, so the time to consider using NVIVO software was at first thought… OMG! Here we go! The idea that I had to learn new software and be good enough to effectively use it to facilitate this data management and coding for my dissertation was overwhelming. My Chair, Dr. Lane was a blessing sent to me, but she had never used NVIVO 12, or any other versions previously. So, I had to learn it. I was on my own with learning how to use the software as a tool.

ONE STEP AT A TIME

The book, "Dissertations and Theses from Start-to-Finish" (2006) by John D. Cone and Sharon L. Foster mentioned, "The fewer the steps between the computer and the raw data, the better off you will be." Knowing how to "code" the data is helpful for the process, but in qualitative studies this data will be more than likely in narrative descriptions such as interviews. Coding is only one aspect of the process, but understanding and interpreting the data requires us to become very intimate with our research. Only you can do that, even with the help of others. This is your research. Own it!

PREPARING THE DATA & CATEGORIES

So, I want you to think of your data coding as the narrative rich descriptions that you collected from your sample population, but let's go a few steps further. These rich descriptions are the deeper context of meaningful data that should have alignment with the research questions formulated in your proposal.

THE MAIN FOCUS

The coding process requires you to consider how effectively these data responses will answer or refute the primary overarching research questions that guide your entire study. Using NVIVO 12 software, the process of organizing the data, will allow you to become more efficient. Most doctoral students have been working diligently to reach the point of data collection in their program, and to now have the chance to code and analyze your data is priceless. There are additional elements that you are required to consider, such as refinement of your themes, and reduction of the data analysis components to better manage the data thematic analysis.

THEMATIC DATA ANALYSIS

To develop your data themes, there are several authors that articulate the proper method for theme development, or *thematic analysis* as it has been described. According to Krippendorff (2004), the modalities of using thematic analysis has its roots in making sense of the texts, which allows the data to answer the research questions. The correct reasoning behind interpreting your data into themes is to determine whether or not these data will answer or refute your "primary research questions". Other authors, such as Ando, Cousins, & Young (2014) mention the process of data collection and analysis in phases. The first phase takes place during the transcribing and analysis of the research data (Ando, Cousins, & Young, 2014). When we complete the transcriptions, this allows us to have engaged the data with a directness of seeking to understand the context of meanings. In the second phase of data analysis, Ando, Cousins, & Young (2014), mentioned the process of organizing and sorting of data can be identified as the "coding" of our qualitative data. It is safe to say that seeking to understand the data and possible themes within the raw data, are crucial in finding and articulating out the thematic data that will answer and/or refute the primary research questions. The data that you have collected will consist of the transcribing and interpretation of the raw data from the direct interview data gathered from your interviews sessions. This allows qualitative researchers to assess and highlight specific areas of the "rich descriptive" content within the raw data for significant passages and phrasings.

THE INDUCTIVE OR DEDUCTIVE PROCESS

There are two methods of performing these types of analyses. This process of data analysis are done inductively or deductively. The inductive process is performed by starting from the data and working up from within the data, versus deductively working from the top down.

The deductive process is done by having the data analysis driven by theory, while the inductive process allows the data to support the research and process. Think of inductive process as building the foundation from the data (ground up), versus the deductive process of using a theory to work from, towards finding thematic elements of interest.

DATA SATURATION

The mention of "theoretical saturation" is highly regarded as a standard in qualitative research data analysis. Saturation occurs when researchers reach the point of no additional themes are found within the data, when reviewing the data extensively in reference to a category of interest (Glasser & Strauss, 1967). The origins of theoretical saturation were developed out of grounded theory, however; the way to differentiate this type of saturation, is by labeling this method "data saturation".

Saturation is "a tool used for measuring research and qualitative data to support dissertation research studies" (Palinkas, Horwitz, Green, Wisdom, Duan, & Hoagwood, 2015). Data saturation occurs when the responses become repetitive in nature across multiple participants and interviews. This is a standard practice for qualitative research and should be a consideration for qualitative researchers, as a means to strengthen and validate the responses and sample population selected in the research study.

Step 1: Coding Data Responses

So you have completed your data collection process and you are ready to use the **NVIVO** data coding software. You can go to the tutorial videos from QSR International. They are helpful, and in fact taught me how to use the software pretty quickly. Where do you begin? I will show you how the software works and what it can do for you to get your data analyzed quickly. Just 7 steps and you will have all of your coding completed and your themes will emerge for analysis and write up. Let's get started.

Open NVivo 12 and Create A Project. Let's create the project with a name only associated with this project. Now let's import your data. I am assuming that you have transcribed your interviews and interpreted them into a word document or .doc format. Word works best for interviews. We need to have them all nicely organized into folders, or at least a folder for us to use.

CLICK ON IMPORT. Importing the data is the most unique part of the NVivo software. This allows us to analyze the data into folders called the FILES location that will hold our transcribed interviews. Save the import location and type of data that you are importing. You will be prompted to select the interviews from where they are saved in your computer. You will have to highlight and import the interviews individually. You cannot select entire folders. When you import the interviews, you will need to create the routing destination of where the transcriptions will be saved.

For importing Data, NVIVO is able to import the following formats: PDF, AUDIO, WORD DOC, and MEDIA FILES. Hard copy books and archival footage cannot be imported, but NVivo can store the links in folders. Here is the look of the folders where you can align the content that you need from data collection: CLICK IMPORT, and watch the interviews upload.

CLICK CREATE NODES. NODES will be the initial themes folder that are created from the manual coding reviews. This allows us to place the coded data into the NODES folders, so that we may explore the rich descriptions of data first hand. You will have to first CREATE NODES that will allow you to form the initial themes that can be used as holders for the coded data. The importing of data consists of having the transcribed interviews already completed after your data collection process has been conducted. Transcriptions should be very detailed and precise to obtain the accurate descriptions of the participant's meanings for us to explore deeper.

CREATE NODES. In the NODES section, you will create NODES from your transcriptions. You typically want to first import the transcribed interviews into the NVIVO 12 software. We will explore that more in depth when we get to that section. For now, let's focus on what you need to get right to importing data. GO TO THE DATA LINK. Go to the top of the page and click on the DATA link.

This will show the choices and format of your data for importing. This way you can edit the errors that you find right inside the NVIVO 12 software. The Ribbon is pictured above and offers another method to access your important sections, such as importing. This section is set up for quick access. I like the ribbon area, because it is easier to see your immediate functions for use.

The key function for importing from this view is the DATA

function. **CLICK the DATA TAB**

Select DOCUMENTS and find them interviews in your

computer. **CLICK OPEN**.

These documents will be in your **FILES** folder. Transcription data in word doc form works best for our purposes of analysis.

You have your interviews in NVIVO 12 now, so we can move to STEP 2 in order to REVIEW THE CODING and find out which themes will emerge initially from within the data.

Step 1 Summary. Step 1 is the coding data responses and transcriptions that have been gathered during the interview process. As part of your ethics agreement, you have coded your participants and kept all data with the highest level of protective management.

These transcribed data are the interpretations of what each participant stated as your interview process took place. Of course, the highlights of their responses will stand out and have more than likely, already become somewhat apparent to you. This is leading us into STEP 2, which is the actual process of "REVIEW THE CODING".

As your interviews continued in the data collection process, several potential themes might have also emerged. It is very common to have some similarities in responses in the data, and as we input these data into NVIVO 12. NODES in Step 2 will now separate the data that you have just imported into NVIVO 12; which are referred to as the INITIAL THEMES. NOW WE GO TO STEP 2.

Step 2: Review the Coding

To review the coding with an effective strategic plan, you will first create folders for your Initial Themes, which are also called stored in the NVIVO folder called NODES.

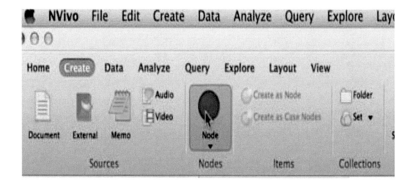

Click NODE and name each NODE based upon your THEMES that were discovered in the data collection. These initial Nodes will be categories within the data analysis portion and at this stage of the journey.

Node Properties

▼ General

Name: Untitled

Description:

☐ Aggregate coding from child nodes   Color:

Location: Nodes ▶

▼ Attribute Values

You can name the **NODE** and assign a color to it in the **Node Properties** section. This will help with your data **Color Stripe** coding section.

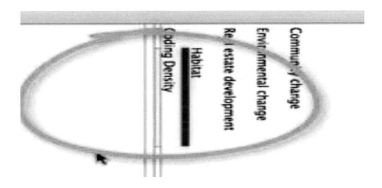

NOTE: If you have formed and asked the correct types of interview questions, then you will notice some elements of your initial themes emerging during the data collection and transcribing. These are not the final themes, but these observations will allow you to examine and consider some of the coding that you will want to consider.

Open the interviews to begin CODING.

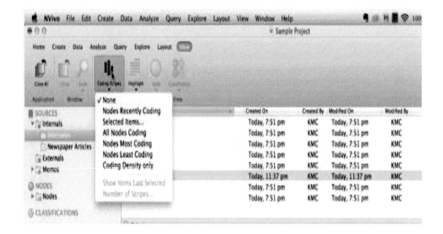

Click **VIEW** then scroll down to select **CODING ALL**

NODES. NVIVO 12 can organize all of your ideas, thoughts,

literature, memos and content. Next, you will click on the **FILES**

section to read a passage from the interviews. You will highlight

that section of interest, and then Drag and Drop it into the

appropriate **NODE** folder that you have labeled as an initial theme.

Name	Sources	Refere...	Created On	Created By	Modified On
Community change	0	0	Today, 11:45 pm	KMC	Today, 11:45 pm
Environmental change	0	0	Today, 11:45 pm	KMC	Today, 11:45 pm
Environmental impacts	0	0	Today, 11:46 pm	KMC	Today, 11:46 pm
Real estate development	0	0	Today, 11:46 pm	KMC	Today, 11:46 pm

Robert

Henry

What do you think about the natural environment Down East? How would you describe that?
What do you like or not like about the environment down there?

Robert

I'm very fond of it. I would hate to see it change significantly. I have mixed feelings about development. I understand there are economic reasons to develop land but I would rather the area stay as it is as much as possible. That doesn't mean I'm 100 percent against construction. But I'm pretty much against high-rise construction, especially the closer you get to the water. I think it ought to be left so that people who were several 100 yards inland will have a view of the water anyway. I hate to see congestion increase. One thing we like about Harkers Island is you don't pass through on your way anywhere. If you're in Harkers Island, you're either lost or that's where you intended to go.

Do this for each interview and participant that has been transcribed. Each of the transcribed sections should be very detailed and completely accurate of the participant's meaningful content. This is only the initial coding process! There is still more work to do to refine these codes into themes. You will have all of your themes now developed and all of your data coded into the proper place for analysis. Each participant's context will be categorized now in a coded format. See the following chart of NODES

Promotional Factors	6	11	Today, 9:50 PM	TLL	Today, 10:53 PM	TLL	●
Challenges	6	10	Today, 9:05 PM	TLL	Today, 10:50 PM	TLL	●
Equal Opportunity	6	9	Today, 9:16 PM	TLL	Today, 10:52 PM	TLL	○
Diversity Initiatives	6	7	Today, 9:07 PM	TLL	Today, 10:51 PM	TLL	●
Qualifications	6	7	Today, 9:18 PM	TLL	Today, 10:52 PM	TLL	●
Educational Value	6	6	Today, 8:52 PM	TLL	Today, 10:49 PM	TLL	●
Influences	6	6	Today, 8:55 PM	TLL	Today, 10:49 PM	TLL	●
Recommendations	6	6	Today, 9:24 PM	TLL	Today, 10:53 PM	TLL	●
Leadership Traits	5	5	Today, 9:20 PM	TLL	Today, 10:53 PM	TLL	●

The coding stripes will come in handy when you look at your themes and also are seeing the data in various graphic depictions. These can be changed or corrected if you make a mistake, so no worries. Each coding will have a color code assigned to it, which you can see in the detail view:

Robert

I'm very fond of it. I would hate to see it change significantly. I have mixed feelings about development. I understand there are economic reasons to develop land but I would rather the area stay as it is as much as possible. That doesn't mean I'm 100 percent against construction. But I'm pretty much against high-rise construction, especially the closer you get to the water. I think it ought to be left so that people who were several 100 yards inland will have a view of the water anyway. I hate to see congestion increase. One thing we like about Harkers Island is you don't pass through on your way anywhere. If you're in Harkers Island, you're either lost or that's where you intended to go.

The colors are to help you identify the patterns and density of the Coding that has taken place. This also is much easier visually.

Step 2 Summary

In summary of Step 2, the Review the Coding; is the process of now finding and noting your Initial Themes from the data, and to determine the quality and accuracy of the data. The process of coding is a matter of first organizing your data from the interviews into folders that are labeled by THEMES (NODES). Each section with common interests becomes a separate THEME based upon the data that emerges from the coding process.

The key is to listen closely, and make sure that you match phrases with themes when you drag and drop each phrase into a NODE (THEME) folder. Qualitative Data is always descriptive so the "coding" is by capturing the written narratives into categories (themes, or nodes) as we engage the data.

Well, of course. If this was the coding of quantitative data with numbers, then we would be capturing numbered data in another software program. You may ask yourself; if qualitative data coding is really this easy? It is "easy" once you know what you are doing, but if you do not have a clue, then it's very complicated. The coding process in NVIVO is designed to manage and organize descriptive data for coding and analysis in your studies. Let's continue to Step 3: Check the Word/ Text Queries. Many of these queries are equally as important for you to explore. The method by which you engage the queries can create new suggestions and ideas for coding and potential theme development.

In the next chapter which is step 3: check the word/text queries; the reason for introducing this chapter is because you can see the journey reach a significant milestone, while also understanding the commitment required to complete your understanding of the data.

STEP 3: TEXT & WORD QUERIES

Step 3 consists of the word frequency as most frequently used by your participants. These can be explored through TEXT QUERIES. TEXT QUERIES are run in NVIVO and will be displayed the number of times and by frequency from each participant.

The interview participants often refer to a category of themes in specific terminology based on the interview questions asked. NVIVO can explore those patterns and phrases most commonly used in your data. Let's begin by Clicking QUERY, then TEXT SEARCH to open the search area.

Type in the word you want to search for (or phrase), and click

RUN QUERY.

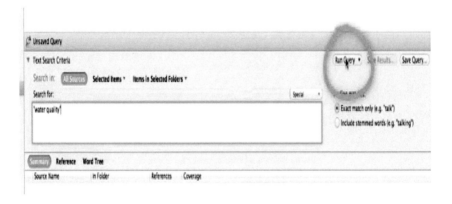

This will show you all of the matches for the word or phrase that you

have searched in this **TEXT QUERY SEARCH**. When you search

for a specific word of phrase, then you can look at it highlighted in the

data passages when clicking on the Nodes in **Detail View.**

VIEWING THE CODING

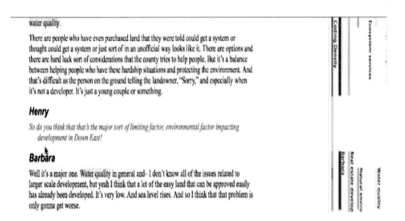

You have several options when looking at your coded references and

TEXT QUERIES. You can view the SUMMARY area, or

REFERENCES area. The Summary area is the overall collection of

where the TEXT QUERY has been used. The references area is

important to access your coded rich descriptions by theme for writing

the analysis section of your dissertation.

Internals\\Interview 1
2 references coded, 8.39% coverage
Reference 1: 4.66% coverage
I received 3 promotions over a period of 14 years. Since I have retired, the pay
increase question does not apply. During my tenure, I was fairly satisfied with the
pay raises. There were times in which I personally felt that money was mismanaged
by the city with employee's benefits and salaries used to balance the budget.
Reference 2: 3.74% coverage
Unfortunately, women wanting to promote rapidly in this organization must do so
by cultivating relationships with the right persons at the right time. Trying to
promote up by hard work and intelligence leads to longer waits, which most are not
willing to do.
Internals\\Interview 10
1 reference coded, 2.06% coverage
Reference 1: 2.06% coverage
1 promotion/10 months; Increased pay within last 5 months; somewhat satisfied
with frequency of raises.
Internals\\Interview 11

NODES SECTION

The nodes section is the detailed collection of the CODED statements that you previously had to drag and drop into each NODE (Theme) folder. For the data analysis section, this will be very helpful for comparison and contrasting.

Now that you have coded all of your data and organized it in NVIVIO 12, the process will be easier to understand. You will enable you to explore the comparison and contrasting for the Findings and Results.

MEMOS AND NOTES

You can use NVIVO 12 in the Memos section to make Notes about your THEMES and DATA. In Step 4 section, we will look at how using NVIVO 12 can support the DATA ANALYSIS section of your Dissertation. STEP 4 is the process by which you can use NVIVO 12 to analyze the large amounts of data content for precise information.

AGGREGATES THE DATA

The software enables researchers to aggregate large amounts of data for comparison and analysis. That is the true benefit of using NVIVO 12 software. In the Step 3 summary, the **TEXT QUERY** is the basis for double checking to make certain that you have developed the THEMES from the DATA.

Through **TEXT QUERY** and **WORD FREQUENCY** searched, you will see the most relevant data that emerges.

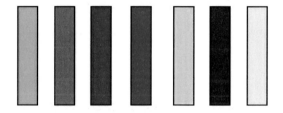

LET'S MOVE TO STEP 4!

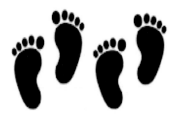

Step 4: Analysis of the Data

Analysis of qualitative data begins with the process of data collection. As you are collecting data by interviews, you should have taken notes to make notes of specific cues and gestures pertaining to the participant responses. In particular, the verbal and physical responses shared with you during the data collection process requires researchers to have a trustworthy analysis process that you must be able to articulate (Newell, Norris, White, & Moules, 2017).

THE PROTOCOL

This process occurs from the time that you start the recording, to transcribing, to developing themes and how these themed data were interpreted. The data analysis will make the writing process more interesting for your findings from the data collection, as you further explore your data within the themes that have emerged. As you check the coding, you can use word frequency query to explore the most common words used by participants. You will want to run the word frequency query to check the Nodes and see what the participants are saying in context. The categories most frequently used will be identified by the number of times they have been mentioned by participants; and in which interview passages.

WORD QUERIES

By clicking the Ribbon Tab, then word frequency, you will see the most frequent words listed from your data. NOTE: Frequency alone is not the deciding factor for coding, but it is good to be familiar with what the data is saying. With NVIVO 12 software, you can set the minimum number of words in the query searches. I recommend checking for several words in sets of 30 20, 15, 10, 9, and so on counting down to at least a minimum of 3.

Try a couple different word/text query amounts to see how the software displays results. Your data will not determine the number of themes that you will finalize for use, but the data will show you several categories for consideration. This is important because you will see your themes emerging in the word/ text query listing when you run queries with NVIVO 12. These words that are listed can also be displayed in a **word cloud.**

Word cloud's make great graphic depictions of word frequency and themes. The Data Analysis technically began with your transcribing of data as it was interpreted and collected from the interview process.

The Data Analysis conducted after the NVIVO 12 CODING will be much more detailed in terms of what the statements are saying. By having everything coded into separate themes and Nodes, the Themes can now be Compared and Contrasted thoroughly.

Data can be analyzed by focusing on a Theme (NODE) one at a time, using the **NVIVO 12** data structuring for management. As you write up the findings and results, you will have the coded data in separated

NODES folders for evaluation. You will be looking at the REFERENCES SECTION area to articulate the comparisons.

Step 4 Summary

In STEP 4, the data analysis was explored to show you how to take a direct approach to using NVIVO 12 to analyze the data. The use of analysis shows the most frequently mentioned areas of the interviews introduced. This allows you to actually see the Initial Themes that emerge from your data. When you run the analysis you will know the coding that align with the research questions which align the study.

INITIAL THEMES

The analysis of the data and writing of the results will be a lot easier to understand as you now have your initial themes and you should be able to see the comparisons and contrasts between all of the participants for refinement and development of the final themes. The transcribing of recorded interviews, interpretations, and manual coding allowed you to live with your data more intimately for repetition, and through this process alone, we are really able to understand it more thoroughly.

LET'S MOVE TO STEP 5

Step 5: Demographics w/ NVIVO 12

Step 5 explores the use of **NVIVO 12 for DEMOGRAPHICS.**

NAME	AGE	GENDER	RACE
James	35-40	M	W
PHIL	41-49	M	B
ROSE	50-55	F	B

By coding the demographic attributes, these data can help you to arrange for your figures and tables in writing the findings and results section of your dissertation. Through organizing your demographic data, we can manage your data under the section that is called **Node Attributes.**

In the same process that you used to code the Nodes and Themes; you

will do the same for the **DEMOGRAPHIC** attributes.

In the Ribbon section, you will find the NODE CLASSIFICATION

CLICK HERE. This will add a folder to the NODES section, but this

folder allows you to separate NODES CLASSIFICATION first.

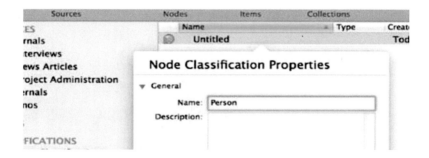

Next you will add the ATTRIBUTES such as gender, age, education,

and other data. In this section you will save the Classification, and then

add the New Attribute. ATTRIBUTES are the DATA that is added

when you click on the classification link, and then add NEW

ATTRIBUTE

Within **NVIVO 12,** you can break down each attribute by **VALUE** and

THEME using the **CASE NODE** option.

A **CASE NODE** is the folder that holds each Participants' attributes;

their statements; and Data which can be separated into **CASE NODE**

sections. **Create Case Nodes.**

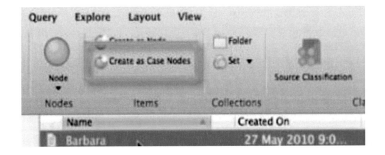

The **CASE NODES** will allow you to put one person's **Attribute**

Data into that **CASE NODE** file.

Person			
Name ▲	gender ▽	community ▽	age group ▽
Barbara	Unassigned	Unassigned	Unassigned
Charles	Unassigned	Unassigned	Unassigned
Dorothy	Unassigned	Unassigned	Unassigned

This is the easiest method for organizing your **Demographics** and **Attributes** data. From a Participant's **NODE** folder, you can add the **CLASSIFICATION Section to that NODE. REPEAT THIS FOR EACH NODE.**

The box below shows the classification

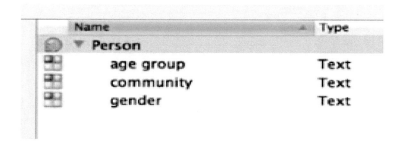

Name	▲ Type
▼ **Person**	
age group	Text
community	Text
gender	Text

The bottom section shows the attributes

Person			
Name ▲	gender ▽	community ▽	age group
Barbara	Unassigned	Unassigned	Unassigned
Charles	Unassigned	Unassigned	Unassigned
Dorothy	Unassigned	Unassigned	Unassigned

In the attributes section, you can **add the specific criteria** for demographics **as needed**. These data can be displayed in various forms of charts and graphs for your write up section of the dissertation.

Step 5 Summary

In Step 5 we explored the **Demographic** data for your study. This allows the coding of demographic data into **Node Attributes.**

The **NODE ATTRIBUTES** are the specific characteristics of a classification within the **CASE Node** data sets. Step 5 explores how to code the data and expand your options using **Case Nodes** as the process for data management. Things can be explored with very meticulous details for the study, while the reason for the seven steps is to provide you with a context and method by which to code your data and arrange it for comparison and analysis.

Step 6: Refine Themes for Writing

In Step 6, the NVIVO 12 software for data coding and analysis has

extra features to use for REFINE your themes. This section is one of

the most productive areas for gathering the data and writing up the

final themes by interpreting the data in depth for selection. Each

theme that has emerged provides us with a unique set of data for

expressing the overall essence of thematic findings. This was STEP 6

to show you that NVIVO 12 does not have to be so complicated.

(SCENARIO DETAILS)

Let's first make up a hypothetical scenario with questions to explore

how some potential themes might emerge. This scenario will explore

the life of a martial artist, and their lived experiences of being able train

with the superstar and Martial Artist (Bruce Lee).

Hypothetical Scenario w/ RQ's are as follows:

Researcher: Question # 1: Can you describe how you felt as a

Martial Arts Instructor the first time that you met and spoke to Bruce Lee?

Participant 1: I felt nervous at first, but then I realize that Mr Lee was a highly trained professional as I myself. When I thought about these truths, then I was able to relax and be humbled by his presence.

Researcher: Question # 2: What about those experiences would you saw were most memorable in terms of training with such a disciplined athlete?

Participant 1: I would say that, the most rewarding experiences were the times that I was able to train with Bruce Lee, while just he and I were warming up in the gym before the film shoot.

This example of the types of research questions are a reminder that you will have to provide a thorough assessment of the data and themes. Through exhaustive research of the literature, the research questions are supported or refuted to tell us about the data. The following initial themes/categories were developed from the research data, as it emerged to address the primary research questions. These themes are listed in the following chart as relevant to some of the coded data which supports the research questions.

Initial Themes/Categories

Qualities of Influence	Athletic Qualities	Recognizable Qualities
Trained Professionals	Career Mentors	Success Traits

The important idea to remember here, is that these themes/ categories will be refined as you engage the data with more rigor. The key is to make sure that you have all of the data in one place for review and assessment. This will allow you to examine it and refine your themes after the coding and analysis of your data.

FOCUS WITH RIGOR

So, the first method to refining your themes is to determine whether or not the data aligns with the research questions. You should use the themes in the NODES folder to help you write out the Refined Themes. Using the NODES area will you to write out a draft of the results and ideas for comparing themes. NVIVO 12 works to your advantage and if you use the NODES for refining the themes to more closely align with the research questions, and it will make the process much easier to manage. The data that you have coded will be the reference data for you to examine for content. The research questions are the guiding elements for the research, and how well the data refutes or supports these research questions to address the answers, will provide us with the details about the significance of the data meanings.

Potential Themes

Qualities of Influence	Athletic Qualities	Recognizable Qualities
Training with Professionals	Career Mentors	Success Traits

The potential themes were aligned to address the research questions. This is the most important area to consider for the research process and guidance, should you forget what the reasoning for conducting this research is all about.

The process to refine these themes into a more concise effort, requires us to interpret the data with a deeper contextual framework. The following figure shows the refined themes example to show how these listed themes can be arranged to provide a more concise presentation.

Refined Themes

Recognizable Qualities of Successful Martial Artists
Understanding the Truest Expressions of Martial Artists

These refined themes give you the ability as a researcher to look more in depth at the initial categories that have been developed; however through this deeper contextual representation you are able to re-define and concisely present the meanings or the essence of meanings. As researchers we are the primary instruments in analyzing all of the data with our expert opinions.

INTERPRETATION OF THE DATA

In providing a clear and unbiased interpretation the data, we are responsible for how we present the data from the study as to share the rich descriptive messages being stated. You may have to truly engage these interpretations of the data, with a sense of patience and humility.

Essentially, you have the most knowledge about the data because you have been fully engaged in the literature and your selected theories. Recalling the evidence of literature, both in the past and present tense, also actively provides you with clarification and memory. Please understand the current scope of empirical data as applicable.

Step 7: Additional Analysis Required

In this newest version of "NVIVO 12 in 7 Steps" I took the liberty to re-align the seven steps to support researchers in a more critical understanding of this entire process. It is crucial and very important that you understand the process of analysis as not being a linear process of completion in scope. There is a higher level of responsibility required along with a developed discipline for seeking to evolve your depths of understandings.

DEEPER CONTEXTUAL UNDERSTANDING

The purpose of a deeper contextual analysis is to further explore the categories on the roof are the things that you have now defined for your research. In order to engage with a deeper understanding you the researcher are the primary instrument, and in accordance with understanding how the data might align with the research, you must have exhausted the research process. Considering whether or not your data introduces new knowledge into the areas of literature, theory, and empirical academia; the deeper rigorous understanding must provide clarity. Your key areas of exploring how effective or ineffectively the data has addressed the research questions is the primary focus of reflection. It is through these considerations and reflections that you will develop the basis for considering whether your data supports or refute your guiding research question associated with the purpose of the study. This comparison and contrasting of the data is your ultimate focus and goal.

MANAGING FEEDBACK IN CONTEXT

Every academic scholar and researcher that has completely dissertation received feedback for just about every draft submission. This is standard practice to improve your research study in writing. You're Chair, committee members, and reviewer's all have a diverse set of background experiences and understandings in reference to doctoral level research, theories, and dissertation level writing. Having engaged the various methodologies with multiple clients on a dynamic range of topics and designs, affords them the respect and credibility to support and constructively review your research. Every intention of your team is to enhance and constructively coordinate your efforts for refinement. Feedback is always a part of the process for improvement. Embrace it, and make the updated corrections as requested.

THE DOCTORAL COMMUNITY

This process is just beginning of your introduction acceptance into the community of higher learning as a top rated and refined academic scholars. As I have my initial meet and greet assessment in interviewing some potential new clients, some of the comments made were: "I just want to be done", or "I'm so tired" and "I'm overwhelmed". These feelings and comments are pretty typical and normal at these final stages of completing your dissertation. As a side note for what I would like for you all to understand as researchers is; yes it has been quite a journey, and yes it is frustrating, and it is challenging. It also at times even seems impossible; but you selected to become better, and to become more, to be more. So guess what? More is expected of you, and more discipline is required of you to respect the community of scholars. You must find and retain a higher level of respect for yourself. Respect the title that you were trying to acquire because this title of "Dr." is not for everyone, but this title is rather for anyone who is completely committed to achieving a matured discipline, which prepares you to deserve the title and all his accolades. You must also be willing to accept the responsibility. With all of that having been said, you should be aware how this status is just the beginning in achieving approval and graduation with a refined and higher level of discipline. The moral to this story is that "there is always more work to be done". Should you choose to hire or engage outside help and support for your deal analysis you could actually disclose this in your non-disclosure agreement with University and make sure your IRB is also fully aware of your intentions and your actions.

THE JOURNEY

As doctoral students, we have all worked very hard to reach this point of the data collection and now the data analysis. Having each collectively spent the long days, nights, and years of research; we have created countless draft after draft after draft of revisions, to reach this point of a masterpiece and body of work. As we now hold a product of our highest level of integrity and achievement, we must make sense of what the data is saying to us. The amazing realization is that we have spent so much time with this data, and it changes over time, that we are now indoctrinated with it in spirit. By the time we reach data analysis there is no one else that could know more about your research study because you have done the comprehensive research and literature reviews with a dedication and perseverance unlike any other project.

THE BEAUTY OF THIS MOMENT

Data Analysis and Coding is the beautiful achievement stage in the journey; which allows you to experience and explore the depth of your research questions and findings. NVIVO 12 will support that process. Each of these steps are the basic process of how to very directly get your data coded and what you need to get from using the software. This process is about working in a timely manner as most students are nearing the completion of their program deadlines.

WHAT NOW?

Now you will begin to write up all of these findings in the proper section, which is normally chapter 4 of the dissertation process. You will literally present the data and exactly what it says from the analysis segment. Each area of themes is crucial to discuss and how the data emerges through your participants and their responses.

HOW TO WRITE UP THE DATA

Take the direct approach to what your coded data speaks about and support the data with recent citations and literature. If there are limited data sources, then use the most recent data to support the need for conducting the study. You are the expert on this topic as you have comprehensively developed this research with a depth of knowledge for contributing and filling your gap in the field of empirical literature.

CHAPTER 4 & 5

Think about writing concisely and clearly in the findings that you have discovered. I personally enjoyed the writing of chapter 4 and chapter 5. Chapter 4 will be strictly what the data says, so it will be filled with a lot of the coded passages of what are commonly called "rich descriptions". These passages should be included from your participants as coded segments based on the responses during interview. You should include enough of the key phrases, but not every line in their responses. Key phrases are nice to include, as they add depth from the participant interviews. The interviewers will let you know if you need more or less of the phrases. When writing out chapter 5 for the study, there will be more of the comparison and contrasting of data for presenting the results segments. I would like to be the first to say that I hope this short book has helped you to understand NVIVO 12 and how the coding process actually works. If you need coaching or assistance from me, please reach out and let me know. I would be happy to assist you in any way that I can do so. Happy analyzing of that data, and congrats to you in advance! See my contact information on the next page!

THANK YOU

FOR ASSISTANCE WITH NVIVO, CONTACT US:

LOONEY CONSULTING GROUP

www.LooneyConsultingGroup.com

" Empowering Minds for Success"

ABOUT THE AUTHOR

Dr. Troy L. Looney has a Doctorate of Management in Organizational Leadership, a Master's of Science in Internet Marketing, and a Bachelor of Arts in Business and Marketing. Dr. Troy Looney is also a Certified Coach, Trainer, and Speaker with the John Maxwell Group. As an expert in phenomenology, Dr. Looney explores and examines the lived experiences of many various aspects of the human condition. The ability to help others with their perspectives and goal achievements is a rewarding process in itself that provides power, confidence, and the foundation of self-learning.

"Expand the ink of a scholar to enhance the lives of others"

Dr. Troy Looney

Bulk Book Purchasing, Speaking, and

Personal or Group Coaching:

For more information on discounts for bulk purchases, contact:

S.T. Publishing House

www.LooneyConsultingGroup.com

" Empowering Minds for Success"

References

Ando, H., Cousins, R., & Young, C. (2014). Achieving saturation in thematic analysis: Development and refinement of a codebook. *Comprehensive Psychology*, *3*, 03-CP.

Castleberry, A., & Nolen, A. (2018). Thematic analysis of qualitative research data: Is it as easy as it sounds?. *Currents in Pharmacy Teaching and Learning*.

Glaser, B. G., & Strauss, A. L. (2017). *Discovery of grounded theory: Strategies for qualitative research*. Routledge.

Nowell, L. S., Norris, J. M., White, D. E., & Moules, N. J. (2017). Thematic analysis: Striving to meet the trustworthiness criteria. *International Journal of Qualitative Methods*, *16*(1), 1609406917733847.

Palinkas, L. A., Horwitz, S. M., Green, C. A., Wisdom, J. P., Duan, N., & Hoagwood, K. (2015). Purposeful sampling for qualitative data collection and analysis in mixed method implementation research. Administration and Policy in Mental Health and Mental Health Services Research, 42(5), 533-544.

Stuckey, H. L. (2015). The second step in data analysis: Coding qualitative research data. *Journal of Social Health and Diabetes*, *3*(1), 7.

Made in the USA
San Bernardino, CA
06 December 2018